Create Your Own Story:

A Guide to writing, finishing and publishing your book

(For middle/high schoolers)

Table of Contents

Introduction	4
Chapter 1: Finding Your Why	5
Chapter 2: Embracing Your Own Story	18
Chapter 3: Crafting Your Story	27
Chapter 4: Navigating the Writing Process	41
Chapter 5: Knowing When to stop Writing:	51
Chapter 6: Editing and Revising Your Manuscript	58
Chapter 7: Overcoming Obstacles and Staying Resilient	69
Chapter 8: Getting Your Book Out There	75
Chapter 9: Celebrating Your Success	79
Conclusion	81

Introduction

Hey there, fellow writers! Welcome to the exciting world of creating your own story. I'm pumped to be here as someone who's written eleven books, and I can't wait to share what I've learned with you. In this book, we're going to dive into all sorts of tips, tricks, and exercises to help you not only start writing but also see your book through to the end.

Let's get real for a second: starting a book can be tough. And knowing when to wrap it up? That's a whole other challenge. Trust me, I've talked to aspiring authors from all over, and these are the big struggles they face. But fear not! That's why I'm here. This book is all about helping you figure out what you want to say and giving you the tools you need to start and finish strong.

So buckle up, because we're about to embark on an awesome journey together: Creating Your Own Story! Let's do this!

Chapter 1

Finding Your Why

Everything in life has a purpose, including writing a book. Purpose is like the fuel that keeps us going, the reason behind everything we do. So, before diving into writing, let's take a moment to understand why we're doing it.

First things first, let's talk about you. Before you can figure out your message, you need to understand yourself. Your purpose starts with knowing who you are at your core. And how do you do that? By identifying your character.

Character is all about the qualities that make you who you are, both mentally and morally. It's about what you stand for and believe in. And where do these beliefs come from? Well, mostly from your experiences.

Think about it: your experiences shape your beliefs. Whether it's stuff from your childhood, things you learned in school, or moments that touched you spiritually, they all play a part in forming your convictions.

Convictions are those strong beliefs you hold onto tightly. They're like the building blocks of your character. And the cool thing is, you have some say in what experiences you're exposed to. Sure, when you're younger, you don't have much control, but as you grow, you can choose what you let into your life.

Now, you might be wondering, "What does all this have to do with writing a book?" Well, stick with me. Remember, a book is basically a bunch of thoughts organized into a message. To know what message you want to share, you've got to understand your purpose first.

I've got a system to help you do just that. It's all about starting from the end and working your way back to the beginning. Begin by asking yourself, "What have I been exposed to?" Your experiences shape your beliefs, and those beliefs form your character. And the right character? That's what helps you live a purposeful life.

So, take a moment to think: What do you need to be exposed to in order to find your purpose? What experiences will help shape your convictions? Once you've got that figured out, you'll be well on your way to discovering your purpose and writing your story with intention.

Answer the following prompt so you can have a resource to go back to in understanding Purpose

1. **Who/What Do You Need to Be Exposed To? (examples below)**

    - A mentor who inspires you
    - Books or podcasts on topics you're passionate about
    - Volunteering in your community
    - Attending workshops or seminars
    - Surrounding yourself with positive and motivated friends

    _____
    _____
    _____

_____
_____
_____
_____
_____
_____
_____
_____
_____
_____
_____
_____

2. **What Experiences Currently Shape My Convictions? (examples below)**

    - Volunteering at a local shelter
    - Overcoming personal challenges
    - Traveling to new places and experiencing different cultures
    - Pursuing hobbies or interests outside of your comfort zone
    - Learning from inspirational stories or role models

_____
_____

_____
_____
_____
_____
_____
_____
_____
_____
_____
_____
_____
_____
_____
_____

3. **What Are Your Top 10 Firmly Held Beliefs About Yourself? (examples below)**

    - I am capable of achieving my goals, no matter the obstacles.
    - I believe in treating others with kindness and respect.
    - I prioritize self-care and personal growth.
    - I am resilient and can bounce back from setbacks.
    - I believe in the power of hard work and determination.

- I am committed to lifelong learning and self-improvement.
- I trust my intuition and follow my instincts.
- I am responsible for my own happiness and success.
- I embrace challenges as opportunities for growth.
- I believe in staying true to my values and principles.

_____

_____

_____

_____

_____

_____

_____

_____

_____

_____

_____

_____

_____

_____

_____

Remember, these principles form the foundation of your character and will guide you in living a purposeful life.

Once you've discovered your purpose, it's time to uncover your message. Your story has the power to impact others positively, but keeping it to yourself could hinder someone else's growth. Before diving into writing, take a moment to reflect on the importance of your message with questions like these:

Think of a time before this when you were struggling: What resources apart from money would have made a difference?

- Reflect on your life 5-10 years ago: Who did you need back then?

_____

_____

- Physically? (Describe the type of person you wished you had back then)

    - Mentally?

_____

_____

_____

_____

_____

_____

_____

_____

_____

    - Financially?

_____

_____

- Spiritually?

- What resources would have made a difference to you five to ten years ago?

  - Financially?

    _____
    _____
    _____
    _____
    _____
    _____
    _____
    _____
    _____
    _____

  - Spiritually?

    _____
    _____
    _____
    _____
    _____

- Physically?

- Emotionally?

___

- Mentally?

___

- If you could go back to yourself 5-10 years ago, what advice would you give?

- What important lessons have you learned that you want to share with others?

_____
_____
_____
_____
_____
_____
_____
_____
_____
_____
_____
_____
_____
_____
_____
_____

By answering these questions, you'll discover what you have to offer to your readers. Often, we look for solutions outside ourselves when, in fact, we already possess what we need. There's a younger version of you who could benefit from your wisdom, and someone out there aspires to be where you are now. Your goal is to find the message in the midst of your life's experiences. Whether you recall challenging times or fond memories, there's someone who can benefit from your story and the lessons you've learned.

Chapter 2

Embracing Your Own Story

We all have a story to tell, and yours is no exception. Whether it's your own journey, the experiences of someone close to you, or simply who you are as a person, your story holds value. Let's dive into some exercises and prompts to help you embrace your story:

1. Identifying Core Themes and Messages:

    - Think about the important events and experiences in your life. What recurring themes do you see popping up?

    _____
    _____
    _____
    _____
    _____
    _____
    _____
    _____

- Consider the lessons you've learned or the insights you've gained from these experiences. What do you want your readers to take away from your story?

- Reflect on the emotions or values that resonate deeply with you. How can you weave these into your story to make it impactful?

_____
_____
_____
_____
_____
_____
_____
_____
_____
_____
_____
_____
_____
_____

Example: One core theme in my story is the journey of self-discovery and identity. Throughout high school, I've been on a quest to figure out who I am and where I fit in. From navigating friendships and relationships to exploring my passions, my story revolves around finding my true self. I want to show through my writing that embracing our uniqueness and staying true to ourselves is the key to happiness and fulfillment.

Example: Another core theme in my story is the importance of friendship and acceptance. During middle school, I went through a lot of ups and downs trying to find my place in the social scene. From making new friends to overcoming conflicts, my story is all about building connections and embracing diversity. I hope to convey through my writing that kindness and empathy are crucial for creating a supportive community.

Uncovering Pivotal Moments and Turning Points:

- Think back on your life and identify moments that really shook things up for you. What were these moments, and how did they change your path?

_____
_____
_____
_____
_____
_____
_____
_____
_____
_____
_____
_____
_____
_____

_____

_____

- Reflect on the challenges or tough times you've faced. How did you tackle them, and what did you learn along the way?

_____

_____

_____

_____

_____

_____

_____

_____

_____

_____

_____

_____

_____

- Consider how these turning points have shaped the way you see the world and where you're headed. How do they fit into the bigger picture of your story?

_____

_____

_____

_____

Example: One pivotal moment in my high school journey was when I decided to audition for the school play. It was totally out of my comfort zone, but I went for it anyway. Through late-night rehearsals and stepping onto that stage, I discovered a side of myself I never knew existed. This experience not only fueled my love for acting but also taught me the value of taking risks and embracing new opportunities.

Example: Another turning point for me in middle school was when I stood up to a bully who was picking on a friend. It was scary, but I knew I had to do something. Standing up for my friend not only stopped the bullying but also showed me the power of courage and standing up for what's right. This moment taught me that even in tough situations, we have the strength to make a difference.

Embracing Authenticity and Vulnerability:

- Take a moment to think about times when you've felt vulnerable or shown your true self. How have these moments impacted who you are and the stories you want to tell?

_____

_____

_____

_____

_____

- Consider any fears or doubts you may have about sharing your story openly. What steps can you take to overcome these and be true to yourself in your writing?

- Reflect on the importance of being honest and transparent with your readers. How can you authentically convey your experiences and emotions through your writing?

Example 1: There have been moments in my life where I've felt vulnerable and unsure, especially when it comes to sharing my personal experiences with others. But I've learned that being vulnerable is key to telling authentic stories. By opening up about my struggles and successes, I can connect with readers on a deeper level and create a genuine emotional impact in my writing.

Example 2: In my college application essay, I chose to share a vulnerable moment from high school—struggling with self-doubt and academic pressure. By being honest about my insecurities, I hope to give admissions officers a real insight into my life beyond grades and activities. Through vulnerability, I aim to show resilience and growth, proving how I've overcome challenges and become a stronger student and person.

Example 3: In my creative writing assignment for English class, I decided to share a personal story about overcoming self-doubt and embracing my talents. By being open about my struggles, I want to connect with my classmates and inspire them to embrace their own strengths. Through honesty and vulnerability, I hope to create a supportive environment where everyone feels accepted and valued.

Remember, your story is your most powerful tool as a writer. Embrace it, be true to yourself, and let your authentic voice shine through in your writing.

Chapter 3

Crafting Your Story

Now that you have a clear idea of why you're writing and what your story is about, it's time to bring it all together by crafting your narrative. In this chapter, we'll cover:

- Picking the right way to tell your story.
- Making characters that stick in your mind and a plot that keeps you reading.
- Making the places in your story feel real and exciting.

Choosing the Best Way to Tell Your Story:

- Think about different ways stories can be told, like going straight from start to finish, jumping around in time, or showing different points of view.
- Try out different ways of writing to see what works best for telling your story's themes and messages.
- Keep your story clear and easy to follow so readers don't get confused.

Try This:

- Think about stories you love from books or movies. What do you like about how they're told? Can you use any of those ideas in your own story?
- Experiment with planning your story using different ways of telling it, like starting from the beginning, adding flash-

backs, or telling parts of it all at once. Which way feels right for what you want to say?

Examples:

Example: As a high school student, I'm writing my story with different timelines. One part follows my life now at school, while the other part goes back to important moments from when I was younger. This way, I can show how things in my past still affect me today.

Example: As a middle schooler, I'm writing a story about friends facing challenges together. I'm telling it in a straight line, with each chapter focusing on something different like friendship or discovering who we are.

Chronological Timeline Example from Different Perspectives:

Perspective of a High School Student: Chronological Timeline:

- Early Childhood (Ages 0-5):
    - Introduction to school and social settings, making first friends, and discovering hobbies and interests.
- Elementary School Years (Ages 6-11):
    - Adjusting to formal education, facing academic challenges, participating in extracurriculars, and forming identity through activities.
- Middle School Transition (Ages 12-13):
    - Entering middle school, adapting to new social dynamics, exploring personal values, and building deeper friendships.
- Middle School Years (Ages 14-15):

- Dealing with puberty, navigating peer relationships, experiencing first romantic feelings, and setting future goals.
- High School Journey (Ages 16-18):
    - Freshman, sophomore, junior, and senior years filled with academic achievements, extracurricular involvement, personal growth, and memorable events like prom and graduation.

Perspective of a Middle Schooler: Chronological Timeline:

- Early Childhood (Ages 0-5):
    - Starting school, making friends, and discovering interests.
- Elementary School Years (Ages 6-11):
    - Adapting to school routines, facing academic challenges, and forming hobbies.
- Middle School Transition (Ages 12-13):
    - Entering middle school, adjusting to new schedules, and forming new friendships.
- Middle School Years (Ages 14-15):
    - Dealing with changes in body and mind, navigating social pressures, and exploring romantic feelings.

By following a chronological timeline from each perspective, you can outline the significant events and milestones that shape your story's narrative arc, providing a clear structure for your storytelling journey.

Crafting Unforgettable Characters

When you're telling your story, you can be the star or invent someone new to take the lead. But remember, it's not just about who they are – it's about what they stand for.

- Make your characters feel real by giving them their own personalities, dreams, and imperfections.
- Dig into their backgrounds, relationships, and inner struggles to make them more interesting and complex.
- Let your characters change and grow as the story unfolds, so readers can really connect with them.

Here's How:

- Write up profiles for your main characters, with details like where they come from, what they're like, and what they want out of life.

_____

_____

_____

_____

_____

_____

_____

_____

_____

- Think about what pushes your characters forward and what holds them back. What challenges do they face, and why?

- Watch how your characters interact and change over time. What conflicts do they run into, and how do these experiences shape who they become?

_____
_____
_____
_____
_____
_____
_____
_____
_____
_____
_____
_____
_____
_____
_____

Examples:

Example: In my memoir, I introduce readers to a bunch of characters who've been a big part of my life. From my family to my best friends and mentors, each one brings their own special insights and experiences to the story, making it richer and more meaningful.

Example: In my story, I've created a bunch of characters that remind me of kids I know from school – you've got your quiet types, your jokesters, and everything in between. As the story goes on, each character goes through their own ups and downs, learning important stuff about friendship, accepting themselves, and bouncing back from tough times.

Practical Example: Developing Memorable Characters

Character Name: Maya Garcia

Background: Meet Maya Garcia, a 16-year-old who recently moved to a new town because of her dad's job. Maya's into art big time – she loves to draw and paint, and it's her way of expressing herself. But with all the changes, Maya feels kinda lost and lonely in her new school.

Personality Traits:

- Introverted: Maya's not the loud, outgoing type. She's more on the quiet side and prefers to keep to herself.

- Artistic: Drawing is Maya's thing. It's where she feels most herself and where she can let her imagination run wild.

- Compassionate: Even though she's dealing with her own stuff, Maya's always there for others. She's got a big heart.

- Insecure: Making friends isn't easy for Maya, and she's always second-guessing herself.

Goals and Motivations:

- Maya just wants to feel like she belongs in her new school. It's tough being the new kid, but she's determined to find her place.

- Art is Maya's passion, and she's not letting anything stop her from pursuing it – even if it means stepping out of her comfort zone.

- More than anything, Maya wants to learn to accept herself, flaws and all, and find the courage to be true to who she really is.

Arc of Development:

- As Maya navigates her new school and joins the art club, she starts to open up and find her voice.
- Through ups and downs, Maya learns to trust herself and embrace her uniqueness.
- By the end of her story, Maya's grown into a stronger, more confident version of herself, ready to take on whatever comes her way.

Character Name: Jamie Chen

Background: Meet Jamie Chen, a 13-year-old science whiz with big dreams of becoming an astronaut. Jamie's super smart, independent, and loves to explore the mysteries of the universe. But being a girl into science isn't always easy, especially when people doubt her abilities.

Personality Traits:

- Curious: Jamie's always asking questions and seeking answers. She's fascinated by the world around her.
- Determined: Nothing can stop Jamie when she sets her mind to something. She's laser-focused on her goal of reaching for the stars.
- Independent: Jamie's not one to wait around for help. She's a go-getter who likes to figure things out on her own.
- Optimistic: Even when things get tough, Jamie stays positive and believes in herself and her dreams.

Goals and Motivations:

- Jamie's dream is to become an astronaut and explore space. She's willing to work hard and defy expectations to make it happen.
- She's motivated by her love for learning and discovery, as well as her desire to inspire other girls to pursue their passions in STEM.
- Jamie's determined to show the world that girls can do anything boys can – and maybe even better!

Arc of Development:

- Throughout her journey, Jamie faces obstacles and doubters, but she never gives up.
- With the support of her mentors and her own determination, Jamie proves that anything is possible with hard work and perseverance.
- By the end of her story, Jamie's not just an aspiring astronaut – she's a role model and a trailblazer, inspiring others to reach for the stars.

Create Engaging Settings

Hey there! Ready to make your story come alive? Let's talk about how you can make your story's settings pop off the page:

- Use lots of details: Describe your settings using all your senses. What do they look, smell, and sound like? The more vivid, the better!
- Think about the world around your story: Consider the time period, culture, and location of your story. Make sure everything fits together and feels real.

- Sets the scene: Your settings can help set the mood and atmosphere of your story. Use them to add depth and meaning to what's happening.

Here are some prompts to help you get started:

- Imagine you're in your story's main settings. What do you see, hear, and smell? How does it make you feel?

_____
_____
_____
_____
_____
_____
_____
_____
_____
_____
_____
_____
_____
_____
_____
_____
_____

- Do some research on the time period or culture of your story's settings. How can you add cool details to make your world feel more authentic?

- Think about how your settings can reflect the themes and emotions of your story. Can you use them to add deeper meaning to what's happening?

_____
_____
_____
_____
_____
_____
_____
_____
_____
_____

Examples:

Example : My story takes place in a high school, but I'm focusing on specific spots like the bustling cafeteria and quiet library. Each place is like a character, adding drama and depth to the story.

Example : In my story, the middle school is like its own little world, full of ups and downs. From the chaotic hallways to the peaceful library, each setting tells its own story and reflects the characters' journeys.

In-depth examples:

Perspective of a High School Student:

Practical Example: Engaging Settings

Settings are super important in high school life. They're like the backdrop for all the cool stuff that happens, from hanging out with friends to discovering new passions. Let's check out some awesome settings from a high schooler's point of view:

1. The School Cafeteria:
    - This place is where it all goes down during lunchtime. It's buzzing with students chatting, eating, and hanging out. From crowded tables to quieter spots, like where Maya likes to chill, the cafeteria shows off all the different groups and vibes in the school.
2. The Art Room:
    - For Maya, the art room is like her creative hideout. It's full of paint, sketchbooks, and other artsy stuff. Here, she gets to express herself and bond with other artsy folks while discovering her love for drawing and painting.
3. The School Auditorium:
    - This is where all the talent shines! From auditions to big performances, the auditorium is where students show off their skills and support each other. It's all about teamwork and putting on a great show.
4. The Local Park:
    - When students need a break from school, they head to the park. It's the perfect spot for picnics, games, or just chilling by the pond. Nature vibes and good times all around!

Perspective of a Middle Schooler:

Practical Example: Engaging Settings

Middle school life is a whirlwind of places and adventures that shape Jamie's journey. Let's dive into some awesome settings from her point of view:

1. The Classroom:
    - Jamie spends a lot of time here, learning and chatting with classmates. It's where all the learning magic happens, with posters and desks filling the room.

2. The Science Lab:

    - This is Jamie's happy place! Filled with science gear, it's where she gets to experiment and explore cool stuff. Science rules here!

3. The School Library:

    - Need a quiet spot to chill? The library's got you covered. Jamie loves escaping here to read and unwind among the shelves of books.

4. The Playground:

    - When it's time for fun, Jamie heads to the playground. It's where friendships are made, games are played, and memories are created.

By using awesome settings like these, you can make your story feel real and exciting, drawing readers into your characters' world and adventures.

Chapter 4

Navigating the Writing Process

Alright, it's time to put your story on paper! Let's dive into how you can tackle the writing process like a pro:

- Establishing a writing routine and setting achievable goals

Key Strategies:

1. Designate a Writing Space: Find a cozy spot where you can focus on writing without distractions, like a corner in your room with a comfy chair and a small desk.

   Example: "I've claimed a cozy corner in my room as my writing spot. It's quiet and distraction-free, perfect for getting into the writing zone."

2. Set Realistic Goals: Break your writing tasks into smaller chunks and set achievable goals for each session or week.

   Example: "This week, I'm aiming to write 500 words every day. It's a manageable goal that'll help me make steady progress."

3. Establish a Routine: Figure out the best time for you to write and stick to it, whether it's early in the morning, during breaks, or in the evenings.

   Example: "I've decided to wake up an hour earlier each morning to write before school. It's become my daily writing routine."

4. Find Your Productive Time: Figure out when you feel most creative and alert, and schedule your writing sessions during those peak hours.

   Example: "I've realized I'm most productive in the evenings, so I've set aside time to write after dinner when I'm feeling inspired."

5. Stay Accountable: Share your writing goals with a friend or join a writing group to stay motivated and on track.

   Example: "I've teamed up with a friend, and we check in with each other weekly on our writing progress. It keeps us accountable and motivated."

Guided Prompts to establish a writing routine:

1. Reflect on Your Writing Habits: When do you feel most creative and productive? Adjust your schedule to prioritize writing during those times.

   Example: "I'm a morning person, so I've started waking up early to write before school. It's when I'm most focused."

2. Define Your Writing Goals: Break down your big writing goals into smaller, manageable tasks.

   Example: "My goal this month is to finish the first three chapters of my story. I'm breaking it down into smaller tasks to tackle each week."

3. Create a Writing Schedule: Set aside specific days and times each week for writing, and stick to it.

   Example: "I've made a weekly schedule with dedicated writing time. It helps me stay consistent."

4. Set Daily or Weekly Targets: Decide how much you want to write each day or week, and track your progress.

   Example: "Today, I'm aiming to write 1,000 words. I'll set a timer and focus until I hit my goal."

5. Accountability and Support: Find someone to share your writing goals with and keep you accountable.

   Example: "I've asked my friend to check in with me regularly about my writing progress. It's nice to have someone cheering me on."

Overcoming Common Writing Challenges:

Overcoming Common Writing Challenges

Key Strategies:

1. Practice Freewriting: Set a timer and write without stopping to overcome perfectionism and get your ideas flowing.

Example: "When I'm stuck, I set a timer and write for 15 minutes non-stop. It helps me stop worrying about making everything perfect and gets my ideas flowing."

2. Take Breaks: Step away from your writing when you're stuck and do something refreshing to clear your mind.

Example: "When I hit a wall in my writing, I take a short walk or do some stretching exercises. It helps me come back with fresh ideas."

3. Explore Different Writing Prompts: Try out different prompts and exercises to spark your imagination and explore new ideas.

Example: "I have a writing journal where I try out different prompts. It's fun to experiment and see where the ideas take me."

4. Seek Inspiration: Surround yourself with things that inspire you, like books, music, or nature.

Example: "When I'm feeling uninspired, I read books or listen to music that gets my creative juices flowing. It helps me get back into the writing groove."

5. Practice Self-Compassion: Be kind to yourself when you're feeling frustrated or doubtful about your writing.

Example: "Instead of being hard on myself for not writing perfectly, I remind myself that it's okay to make mistakes. I'm learning and growing with each word I write."

Guided Prompts:

1. Identify Your Writing Blocks: Figure out what challenges you face when writing, like perfectionism or lack of inspiration.

Example: "I struggle with perfectionism, so I'm learning to let go and just write without worrying about getting everything right the first time."

2. Explore Creative Exercises: Experiment with different exercises to overcome writer's block and generate new ideas.

Example: "When I'm stuck, I try writing prompts to kickstart my creativity. It helps me think outside the box and come up with fresh ideas."

3. Seek Inspiration: Find what inspires you, whether it's books, nature, or music, and use it to fuel your writing.

Example: "Nature inspires me, so I take walks or sit outside to get inspired. It helps me come up with new ideas for my writing."

_____
_____
_____
_____
_____
_____
_____
_____
_____
_____
_____
_____
_____
_____
_____
_____

4. Practice Self-Compassion: Be gentle with yourself when you're feeling stuck or doubtful about your writing.

Example: "Instead of being hard on myself for not writing perfectly, I remind myself that it's okay to take breaks and come back later. Writing is a process, and I'm learning along the way."

By using these strategies, you'll be able to overcome common writing challenges and keep making progress on your writing journey.

_____
_____
_____
_____
_____
_____
_____
_____
_____
_____
_____
_____
_____
_____
_____
_____

5. Trying Different Ways to Take Breaks: What do you do to relax and refocus when you're feeling overwhelmed or stuck while writing? How can you fit these activities into your schedule to help you stay creative?

Example: "When I'm feeling stressed or stuck while writing, I like to take short breaks to do something fun like going for a walk, listening to music, or even doodling. These little breaks help me clear my mind and come back to my writing feeling refreshed and ready to tackle the next challenge."

_____
_____
_____
_____
_____
_____
_____
_____
_____
_____
_____
_____
_____
_____
_____
_____
_____
_____
_____

Using Tools and Techniques to Stay Organized and Inspired:

1. Try Writing Software: Check out writing apps or software that can help you keep your ideas organized, plan your story, and track your progress.

Have you used any writing apps or software before? How did they help you stay on track with your writing? Are there any new tools you're curious to try?

Example: "I've started using Scrivener for my writing projects. It lets me plan out my story, keep track of my characters, and move scenes around easily."

2. Make an Outline: Create a detailed outline or plan for your writing project to give you a roadmap as you write.

What important events or themes do you want to include in your story? How can you organize them into a clear outline?

Example: "Before I started writing my novel, I made a detailed outline with all the major plot points and character arcs. It helps me stay focused and not get lost while writing."

3. Set Deadlines: Decide on deadlines for different parts of your writing project to help you stay on track and motivated.

What deadlines do you want to set for yourself, like finishing your first draft or revising certain chapters? How will you make sure you stick to them?

Example: "I've given myself six months to finish the first draft of my novel. To make sure I stay on target, I've divided the writing process into smaller goals with deadlines for each one."

4. Celebrate Achievements: Take time to celebrate your progress and successes, whether it's hitting a word count goal or finishing a chapter.

How will you reward yourself for reaching milestones in your writing journey? How can you keep yourself feeling positive and motivated?

Example: "Whenever I finish a chapter or reach a word count goal, I treat myself to something small like a favorite snack or taking a break to watch a show I like. It keeps me feeling motivated and excited to keep going."

5. Stay Connected: Join writing groups or online communities to connect with other writers, share advice, and get support when you need it.

Have you joined any writing groups or communities before? How did they help you with your writing? What kinds of groups would you like to join in the future?

Example: "I'm part of an online writing community where I can talk to other writers, get feedback on my work, and join writing challenges. It's really helped me stay motivated and inspired, especially when I'm feeling stuck."

By using these strategies, you'll not only make progress with your writing but also feel more confident and excited about sharing your stories with others.

Chapter 5

Knowing When to stop Writing:

Think of writing like having a conversation. Just like when you talk to someone, you share your thoughts to get a message across. And once you've said what you needed to say, you stop talking and wait for a response. This same idea applies to writing a book. The key is to use a method called the Work Backwards Method (W.B.M).

Here's how it works:

1. What's my main message?

_____

_____

_____

_____

_____

_____

_____

2. What's the main point I want to make in this chapter or section?

3. Have I made that point clear in this chapter or section?

4. What's the big idea of my whole book?

5. Does my book as a whole get that idea across?

6. Does this chapter or section help emphasize the main idea of my book?

7. Have I clearly stated the message I'm trying to get across?

8. Have I covered everything I need to in this specific chapter or section?

_____
_____
_____
_____
_____
_____
_____
_____
_____
_____
_____
_____
_____
_____

By using this method, you can make sure your writing stays focused and on track, and you'll know exactly when to stop writing because you'll have said what you needed to say.

Chapter 6

Editing and Revising Your Manuscript

Once the initial draft is complete, it's time to refine and polish your manuscript. This chapter will cover:

- Strategies for self-editing and revising your work.
- Seeking feedback from beta readers and critique partners.
- Working with professional editors to enhance the quality of your manuscript.

Through meticulous editing and revision, you'll transform your rough draft into a polished masterpiece.

Strategies for Making Your Book Even Better:

1. **Take a Breather:** Finish your book? Awesome! Now, give yourself a break for a few days or weeks. Stepping away helps you see your story with fresh eyes when you come back to it.

2. **Read It Out Loud:** Want to catch mistakes? Read your book out loud or use a text-to-speech tool. Hearing your words can help you spot weird sentences or grammar goofs that slipped by.

3. **Fix the Flow:** Check how your story flows from one part to the next. Make sure it all makes sense, transitions smoothly, and keeps your readers hooked from start to finish.

4. **Keep It Consistent:** Check that your characters, settings, and plot details stay the same throughout your book. Nobody likes a story where things suddenly change without explanation!

5. **Trim the Fat:** Cut out any extra stuff that doesn't really add to your story. Shorter sentences and fewer words make your writing sharper and more exciting to read.

6. **Make Dialogue Pop:** Check if your characters' conversations sound real and move the story forward. Make sure your tags (like "he said" or "she whispered") are clear and in the right spots.

7. **Polish Your Words:** Make sure your writing is clear, strong, and sounds cool. Swap out boring words for better ones, mix up your sentence styles, and get rid of any tired phrases.

8. **Hunt for Errors:** Read through your book a bunch of times to catch any spelling, grammar, or punctuation mistakes. Use online tools, but don't forget to go over it yourself too!

9. **Get Some Feedback:** Share your book with friends, family, or writing buddies for their thoughts. Listen to what they say and think about how you can make your story even better.

10. **Take It Easy:** Don't stress too much! Editing can be tiring, so take breaks to keep yourself fresh. Come back to your book feeling recharged and ready to make it awesome.

Questions to Guide Your Editing Adventure:

1. **Check Your Book's Bones:** Is your story's overall structure working well, or does it need some tweaking to make it clearer and more exciting?

2. **Meet Your Characters:** How well do you know your characters? Do they feel like real people with their own quirks and dreams?

3. **Listen to Your Story's Voice:** Does your story sound like you want it to? Is the way it's told consistent and fitting with the mood of your tale?

4. **Find the Weak Spots:** What parts of your book do you think need the most work? Focus on those areas to make your story shine.

5. **Unravel Your Book's Theme:** What big ideas is your story exploring, and are they coming through loud and clear?

6. **Seek Out Some Outside Opinions:** Who can give you honest feedback on your writing? Look for different perspectives to help you see your book in new ways.

7. **Make a Plan:** How are you going to tackle your editing? Set some goals and figure out how to reach them step by step.

8. **Search for Errors Like a Pro:** What's your game plan for catching those sneaky mistakes? Develop a system to make sure nothing slips through the cracks.

9. **Stay Strong and Keep Going:** How will you keep your spirits up when things get tough? Remember to celebrate the progress you're making along the way!

Practical Strategies:

1. **Ask a Friend:** Get a classmate or friend to read your story and give you feedback. Sometimes, they notice things you might have missed!

2. **Take It Step by Step:** Don't try to fix everything at once. Focus on one thing at a time, like fixing mistakes, making your characters stronger, or improving the flow of your story.

3. **Use Tools:** Use tools like spell check or grammar check on your computer to help you find mistakes. It's like having a little helper to catch things you might have missed!

4. **Read Out Loud:** Reading your story out loud can help you find places where the words don't sound quite right or where you've repeated the same thing too many times.

5. **Take Breaks:** Editing can be tiring, so take breaks when you need them. It's okay to step away from your story for a little while and come back to it later with fresh eyes.

Guided Prompts:

1. *Find the Oopsies:* What parts of your story do you think need fixing? Are there words spelled wrong, sentences that don't make sense, or places where the story feels confusing?

2. *Set Little Goals:* What do you want to fix first? Maybe start with spelling mistakes, then move on to making your characters stronger or making your story flow better.

3. *Listen Up:* Can you read your story out loud to yourself or someone else? Do any parts sound weird or hard to understand? Those might be places you need to fix!

4. *Ask a Buddy:* Can you get a friend or family member to read your story and tell you what they think? They might have some good ideas for how to make it even better!

5. *Take Breaks:* Editing can be boring sometimes, so it's okay to take breaks. Step away from your story for a little while and do something fun, then come back to it when you're ready.

Chapter 7

Overcoming Obstacles and Staying Resilient

The journey of writing a book is not without its challenges. In this chapter, we'll discuss:

- Strategies for overcoming common obstacles and setbacks.

- Cultivating resilience and perseverance in the face of adversity.

- Seeking support from fellow writers and mentors to navigate challenges effectively.

Writing is a journey, and it is one that can be very challenging. Many aspiring authors start this journey but find it very difficult to finish, which is why I have provided guided prompts and key strategies that will aid you in overcoming obstacles and staying resilient through this journey.

Practical Strategies:

For Middle/High School Students Practical Tips:

1. Recognize Your Feelings: It's normal to feel frustrated or stressed while writing. Acknowledge how you're feeling and remember it's okay to have ups and downs.

2. Take It Step by Step: Break down your writing tasks into smaller, manageable steps. Focus on completing one thing at a time, and celebrate each little victory!

3. Take Care of Yourself: Don't forget to get enough sleep, eat well, and take breaks when you need them. Keeping yourself healthy and happy will give you the strength to face any challenge.

4. Learn from Mistakes: When things don't go as planned, see them as opportunities to learn. Figure out what went wrong, learn from it, and use that knowledge to do better next time.

5. Ask for Help: Reach out to friends, teachers, or online writing communities when you need support. Having people to lean on can make tough times easier to handle.

Guiding Questions:

1. Identify Tough Spots: What parts of writing do you find challenging? How do they affect your progress?

_____

_____

_____

_____

_____

_____

_____

_____

_____

_____

_____

2. Find Coping Strategies: What do you usually do when you're feeling stuck or stressed with writing? Are there new methods you could try?

3. Reflect on Tough Times: Think back to a time when writing felt really hard. How did you manage to push through? What strengths did you rely on?

_____
_____
_____
_____
_____
_____
_____
_____
_____
_____
_____
_____

4. Seek Support: Who can you turn to when you need help with your writing? How can you let them know you're struggling and ask for support?

_____
_____

_____

_____

_____

_____

_____

_____

_____

_____

_____

_____

_____

5. Set Goals: How can you keep going when things get tough? How will you take care of yourself, break tasks into smaller steps, and ask for help if needed?

_____

_____

_____

_____

_____

_____

_____

_____

_____

_____

_____

_____

_____

By using these tips and reflecting on these questions, you'll be better equipped to handle challenges while writing and come out stronger in the end. Remember, tough times don't last forever, and with the right support and mindset, you can overcome anything!

Chapter 8

Getting Your Book Out There

So, you've finished writing your book – congrats! Now it's time to get it out into the world. Here's what you need to do:

1. Revise and Edit: Before you publish, make sure your book is in top shape. Get feedback from others and consider hiring a professional editor to polish it up.

2. Formatting: Get your manuscript ready for publishing by formatting it correctly. This means making it look nice and professional, with things like a title page, copyright info, and consistent layout.

3. Choose Your Path:

    - Traditional Publishing: Send your manuscript to literary agents or publishers and hope they like it enough to publish it for you. They'll handle everything from editing to marketing.

    - Self-Publishing: Take control and publish your book yourself through platforms like Amazon. You'll do all the work, but you get to keep more control and profits.

    - Hybrid Publishing: A mix of both, where you pay a publisher to help with things like editing and design, but you still have more control than with traditional publishing.

4. Cover Design: Create a cool cover that grabs people's attention. You can do it yourself or hire someone to make it look really professional.

5. ISBN and Copyright: Get a special code for your book (ISBN) and consider copyrighting it to protect your work.

6. Distribution: Decide how you want to get your book to readers – through bookstores, online platforms, or even selling it directly on your own website.

7. Marketing: Plan how you'll tell people about your book. This could be through social media, events, or getting reviews from bloggers.

8. Launch Day: Set a date to release your book and tell everyone about it! Get the word out on your website, social media, and anywhere else you can.

9. Keep Track: Watch how your book is doing – how many copies you're selling and what people are saying about it. Use this info to make your marketing even better.

10. Keep Writing: Don't stop now – keep writing and sharing your stories with the world. Publishing your first book is awesome, but there's always more to write!

Here are some helpful resources that I've personally used:

1. Revision and Editing:

    - **Reedsy**: This site has a bunch of professional editors who know different types of writing. You can look through their profiles, ask for prices, and hire someone to help make your writing better.

    - **Fiverr**: Just like Reedsy, Fiverr also has a bunch of editors. You can find someone who fits your style and budget to help you polish your work.

- **Scribendi**: These folks offer editing services for writers. They can help with things like grammar, spelling, and making your writing sound better.
- **Grammarly**: It's like having a smart friend who checks your writing for mistakes and gives you tips on how to make it clearer and smoother.

2. Formatting:

- **Kindle Create**: This is a free tool from Amazon that helps you get your book ready to publish for Kindle or in print. It guides you through the process so your book looks good on any device.
- **Reedsy Book Editor**: Another free tool that helps with formatting your book for digital and print. It's easy to use and gives you lots of options to make your book look just right.
- **Vellum**: This one you have to pay for, but it's worth it. Vellum helps you make your book look super professional, whether it's for ebooks or print.
- **Fiverr**: You can also find people on Fiverr who can help format your book for you at a good price.

3. Choose Your Publishing Route:

- **QueryTracker**: If you're looking to go the traditional route, QueryTracker can help. It has a bunch of info on literary agents and helps you keep track of who you've contacted.
- **Amazon Kindle Direct Publishing (KDP)**: This is where you can publish your book yourself on Amazon. You get to be in control of everything and earn money for each sale.

- **IngramSpark**: Another self-publishing option that helps you get your book out there in both digital and print formats.

4. Cover Design:

    - **Canva**: This is an easy-to-use design tool where you can make your own book cover without breaking the bank.

    - **99designs**: If you want something more pro, you can run a contest on here and get a bunch of designers to create covers for you to choose from.

    - **Reedsy** and **Fiverr**: Both of these sites also have designers who can help you create a custom cover for your book.

5. ISBN and Copyright:

    - **Bowker Identifier Services**: This is where you can get an ISBN, which is like a social security number for your book. It helps identify your book and track sales.

    - **U.S. Copyright Office**: Here you can register your book to make sure your work is legally protected.

    - **Copyright Clearance Center**: If you need to use someone else's work in your book, these guys can help you get permission and pay any fees.

These tools and services can be super useful as you work on getting your book out into the world!

Chapter 9

Celebrating Your Success

I am a firm believer on celebrating while on the journey, and celebrating after you complete your journey. There is absolutely nothing wrong with a pat on the back during and after completing a journey such as writing a book.

As you reach the final stages of completing your book, it's important to celebrate your achievements. This chapter will guide you in:

- Acknowledging and celebrating milestones along the way.
- Reflecting on your growth and accomplishments as an author.
- Planning for the launch and promotion of your book to share your story with the world.

Remember, completing a book is a significant achievement worthy of celebration.

Here are proven key implementation strategies that will guide you in celebrating your success

Perspective of an High Schooler/ Middle schooler

1. **Celebrate Your Wins:** Break your writing journey into smaller goals, like finishing chapters or hitting word counts. When you achieve these goals, take a moment to celebrate! Treat yourself to something nice or share your progress with friends and family.

2. **Keep a Writing Journal:** Start a journal to jot down your thoughts and feelings about writing. Reflect on what you've learned, the challenges you've overcome, and any cool ideas that come to mind. It's like keeping a diary of your writing adventures!

3. **Track Your Progress:** Take screenshots or photos of your writing progress, like your word count or any outlines you've made. Seeing how far you've come can be really motivating and help you stay focused on your goals.

4. **Plan Your Book Launch:** Start thinking about how you'll share your book with the world. Look into different ways to launch and promote it, like sharing sneak peeks on social media or reaching out to bloggers for reviews.

5. **Get People Excited:** Build hype for your book by sharing updates and teasers on social media. Engage with your followers and ask for their input. The more excited people are about your book, the more likely they'll want to read it!

6. **Team Up with Others:** Collaborate with other writers or bloggers to help each other out. You can share each other's work on social media or team up for events. It's a great way to reach new readers and make friends in the writing community.

7. **Party Time:** Once your book is out there, take a moment to celebrate! Throw a launch party, treat yourself to a special meal, or just pat yourself on the back for a job well done. You've worked hard, and you deserve to celebrate your success!

By following these steps, you'll not only celebrate your achievements as a writer but also get ready to share your awesome book with the world!

Conclusion

Congratulations, aspiring authors, on embarking on the journey of creating your own story. By following the techniques, strategies, and exercises outlined in this book, you are fully equipped to write and finish your book.

Remember, you have something valuable to offer to the world, and your story deserves to be told. Embrace your unique voice, unleash your creativity, and let your story shine bright. Go and CREATE YOUR OWN STORY, I cannot wait to hear it!